Trumpet II in B♭

HYMNS FOR BRASS

arranged for brass quintet
by Rick Walters

easy level

THE CANADIAN
BRASS

CANADIAN
BRASS
SERIES OF
COLLECTED QUINTETS

Ah, Holy Jesus

2nd B♭ TRUMPET

Johannes Crüger
("Herzliebster Jesu")

Christ the Lord is Risen Today

2nd Bb TRUMPET

from *Lyra Davidica,* 1708

Eternal Father, Strong to Save

2nd Bb TRUMPET

John B. Dykes, c. 1861

Beautiful Savior

2nd B♭ TRUMPET

Silesian Melody
(Schönster Herr Jesu)

Copyright © 1990 by HAL LEONARD PUBLISHING CORPORATION
International Copyright Secured   ALL RIGHTS RESERVED

A Mighty Fortress

2nd B♭ TRUMPET

Martin Luther, 1529

We Gather Together

2nd Bb TRUMPET

Netherlands Folk Song, 1626

C A N A D I A N B R A S S

SERIES OF
COLLECTED QUINTETS

HYMNS FOR BRASS

arranged for brass quintet
by Rick Walters

contents

Welcome to the new *Canadian Brass Series of Collected Quintets*. In our work with students we have for some time been aware of the need for more brass quintet music at easy and intermediate levels of difficulty. We are continually observing a kind of "Renaissance" in brass music, not only in audience responses to our quintet, but to all brass music in general. The brass quintet, as a chamber ensemble, seems to have become as standard a chamber combination as a string quartet. That could not have been said twenty-five years ago. Brass quintets are popping up everywhere — professional quintets, junior and senior high school ensembles, college and university groups, and amateur quintets of adult players.

We have carefully chosen the literature for these collected quintets, and closely supervised the arrangements. Our aim was to retain a Canadian Brass flavor to each arrangement, and create attractive repertory designed so that any brass quintet can play it with satisfying results. We've often remarked to one another that we certainly wish that we'd had quintet arrangements like these when we were students!

Happy playing to you and your quintet.

U.S. $7.99

— THE CANADIAN BRASS

HL50488755

HAL•LEONARD®
CORPORATION
7777 W. BLUEMOUND RD. P.O. BOX 13819 MILWAUKEE, WI 53213

ISBN-13: 978-1-4584-0155-7
Distributed By
HAL LEONARD

50488755